Maths

Key Stage 1

Revision Guide

Steve Mills and
Hilary Koll

Welcome to this book

What this book is for

This book will help you to revise for the maths tests at the end of Year 2. It will also help you to get better marks in the tests.

What you will need

- Paper, a pencil, crayons and an eraser.
- An adult to check your answers to the **Test yourself!** questions (or you can check them yourself).

How the book is set out

There are some pages of notes about each maths topic. These pages will remind you of what you have already learned at school.

How to work through a topic

- Turn to the topic and read about it.
- Study each example.
  Think about how you would do it on your own.
- Some of the words are in orange.
  The Glossary on pages 62 and 63 tells you what they mean. Try to remember the orange words and their meanings.
- The **Remember** box lists important things that you need to know. Read it. Then cover it. What did it say? Can you remember?
- Read the **Test yourself!** questions. Write your answers on a piece of paper. Ask an adult to check them against the right answers (pages 56 to 59), or you could check them yourself.
- Did you get some questions wrong? Read the topic again. Then have another go.
- Did you get all the questions right?
  Tick the circle in the corner of the page. Well done!

What to do next

- Move on to another topic.
  Carry on until you have worked through them all.
- Look at the tick circles. Are there any that you haven't ticked? Work through those topics again.
- Read the 'Tips for tests' at the back of this book.
  Then you are ready for the tests. Good luck!

How to get even better marks!

Try the Schofield & Sims Maths Practice Papers for Key Stage 1.

Contents

Note for teachers and parents

The Schofield & Sims Revision Guides have been written by teachers, for use at school and at home. The Guides enable children to revise independently for the National Curriculum Key Stage tests (SATs). The focus is on clear explanations of the topics covered by the tests, all of which will already have been taught in school. Each maths topic is matched to the National Numeracy Strategy, and all the curricular links are listed in the Curriculum chart on pages 60 and 61. Practice Papers designed to accompany this book will further improve children's test results (see back cover for full details).

Numbers and their digits

Digits

Each number is made from one or more digits.

This number has one digit.   9

This number has two digits.   2 7

This number has three digits.   3 5 4

Numbers in digits and in words

Look at these numbers written in digits and words:

1	2	3	4	5	6	7	8	9	10
one	two	three	four	five	six	seven	eight	nine	ten

11	12	13	14	15	16	17	18	19	20
eleven	twelve	thirteen	fourteen	fifteen	sixteen	seventeen	eighteen	nineteen	twenty

21	22	23	24	25	26	27	28	29	30
twenty-one	twenty-two	twenty-three	twenty-four	twenty-five	twenty-six	twenty-seven	twenty-eight	twenty-nine	thirty

Other numbers include:

40	50	60	70	80	90	100	200	300	... and so on
forty	fifty	sixty	seventy	eighty	ninety	one hundred	two hundred	three hundred	

1000	2000	3000	... and so on
one thousand	two thousand	three thousand	

Test yourself!

1 Write these numbers in words:
a) 12
b) 24
c) 36
d) 84
e) 18
f) 48
g) 100

2 Write these numbers in digits:
a) thirteen
b) sixty
c) fifty-two
d) seventy-six
e) ninety-five
f) eleven
g) two hundred

Remember

Watch out for difficult spellings like **eight**, **eighteen**, **eighty**, **forty** and **ninety**.

Odd and even numbers

Look at these shoes.

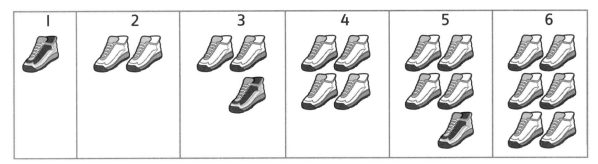

| 1 | 2 | 3 | 4 | 5 | 6 |

- Notice that the numbers 1, 3 and 5 have an odd number of shoes. 1, 3 and 5 are called **odd numbers**.

- Notice that the numbers 2, 4 and 6 have pairs of shoes and no odd ones. 2, 4 and 6 are called even numbers.

Every whole number is either even or odd.

Even numbers

2, 4, 6, 8, 10, 12, 14, 16, 18, 20 … are all even numbers. Any number that is divided by 2 without a remainder is an **even** number.

Is the number 16 even?

16 ÷ 2 = 8

There is no remainder.
So **16** is an **even** number

All **even** numbers end in **0, 2, 4, 6** or **8**.

Odd numbers

1, 3, 5, 7, 9, 11, 13, 15, 17, 19 … are all odd numbers. Any number that is divided by 2 and has a remainder of 1 is an **odd** number.

Is the number 17 odd?

17 ÷ 2 = 8 remainder 1

There is a remainder.
So **17** is an **odd** number

All **odd** numbers end in **1, 3, 5, 7** or **9**.

Test yourself!

1 Say whether each number is odd or even:
   a) 6
   b) 3
   c) 9
   d) 12
   e) 18
   f) 25
   g) 54
   h) 67
   i) 98

2 Which of these numbers are odd?
   123, 566, 462, 388, 482, 698, 659, 597, 365, 471, 600

Remember

All **even** numbers end in 0, 2, 4, 6 or 8.

All **odd** numbers end in 1, 3, 5, 7 or 9.

Counting in ones

Use this 100 square to help you count on and back.

Point to the numbers as you say them aloud.

1	2	3	4	5	6	7	8	9	10
11	12	13	14	15	16	17	18	19	20
21	22	23	24	25	26	27	28	29	30
31	32	33	34	35	36	37	38	39	40
41	42	43	44	45	46	47	48	49	50
51	52	53	54	55	56	57	58	59	60
61	62	63	64	65	66	67	68	69	70
71	72	73	74	75	76	77	78	79	80
81	82	83	84	85	86	87	88	89	90
91	92	93	94	95	96	97	98	99	100

Counting in ones

- Point to number 1. Count slowly in ones, pointing to each number as you say it. How far can you count forwards?

  1, 2, 3, 4, 5, 6, 7, 8, 9 ...

- Try counting backwards. Start from the number 55 and count backwards in ones. How far can you count backwards?

  55, 54, 53, 52, 51, 50, 49 ...

Finding the next numbers in the pattern

- Keep counting on or back to find the next three numbers in the pattern.

  17, 18, 19, 20, ..., ..., ...,

  ↑   ↑   ↑

Test yourself!

1 Count on in ones from 46 to 73.

2 Count back in ones from 96 to 68.

3 Find the next three numbers in these patterns:

   a) 36, 37, 38, 39, ..., ..., ...,

   b) 73, 72, 71, 70, ..., ..., ...,

   c) 85, 86, 87, 88, ..., ..., ...,

   d) 100, 99, 98, 97, ..., ..., ...,

Remember

Practise counting on and back in ones from any number up to 100.

Counting in twos

Counting **every other number** is called **counting in twos**.

- Count forwards **in twos** from the number 2.

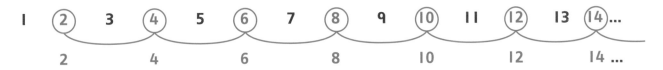

- You can **begin on any number**.

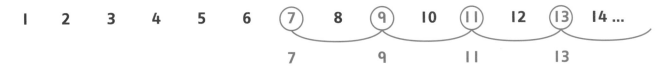

- Now try **counting backwards in twos**, like this ...

32, 30, 28, 26, 24, 22, 20, 18, 16 ...

63, 61, 59, 57, 55, 53, 51, 49, 47 ...

Odd and even numbers

Counting in twos from an odd number

Notice that when you **count in twos**, starting from an odd number, all the numbers will be **odd**.

5, 7, 9, 11, 13, 15, 17, 19 ...

55, 53, 51, 49, 47, 45, 43 ...

Counting in twos from an even number

When you **count in twos**, starting from an even number, all the numbers will be **even**.

4, 6, 8, 10, 12, 14, 16, 18 ...

78, 76, 74, 72, 70, 68, 66 ...

See page 5 for more about odd and even numbers.

Test yourself!

1 Count on in twos from 46 to 76.

2 Count back in twos from 53 to 37.

3 Find the next three numbers in these patterns:

a) 36, 38, 40, 42, ..., ..., ...,

b) 75, 73, 71, 69, ..., ..., ...,

c) 81, 83, 85, 87, ..., ..., ...,

d) 100, 98, 96, 94, ..., ..., ...,

Remember

Practise counting on and back in twos from any number up to 100.

Counting in tens

When you **count in tens**, the **unit** digit **always stays the same**.

In this 100 square, numbers are in **rows of ten**. Look down a column when counting on in tens.

When you **count on from 6**, the unit digit is always 6.

1	2	3	4	5	6	7	8	9	10
11	12	13	14	15	16	17	18	19	20
21	22	23	24	25	26	27	28	29	30
31	32	33	34	35	36	37	38	39	40
41	42	43	44	45	46	47	48	49	50
51	52	53	54	55	56	57	58	59	60
61	62	63	64	65	66	67	68	69	70
71	72	73	74	75	76	77	78	79	80
81	82	83	84	85	86	87	88	89	90
91	92	93	94	95	96	97	98	99	100

Counting on in tens

When you **count on** in tens, the tens digit **grows by one** each time.

The tens digit gets one larger and the unit digit stays the same.

```
  T U
  5 2
+ 1 0
-----
  6 2
```

Counting on from 6

Use the number square to **count on in tens from 6.** You will see that the unit digit is always 6:

6, 16, 26, 36, 46, 56...

Counting on from 2

Now find the column starting with the number 2 and **count on in tens from 2**:

2, 12, 22, 32, 42, 52 ...

Counting back in tens

When you **count back** in tens, the tens digit **gets smaller by one** each time.

The tens digit gets one smaller and the unit digit stays the same.

```
  T U
  5 2
- 1 0
-----
  4 2
```

Test yourself!

1 Count on in tens from 26 to 96.

2 Count back in tens from 87 to 7.

3 Find the next three numbers in these patterns:

 a) 38, 48, 58, 68, ..., ..., ...,

 b) 99, 89, 79, 69, ..., ..., ...,

 c) 31, 41, 51, 61, ..., ..., ...,

 d) 44, 54, 64, 74 ....., ..., ...,

Remember

When you **count in tens**, the **unit digit** always **stays the same**.

Counting in fives

Counting in fives from 5

When counting in fives, notice the pattern in the unit digits.

Counting on in fives from 5

5, 10, 15, 20, 25, 30, 35, 40 ...

Each of these numbers is a multiple of 5, in other words they are numbers in the 5 times table or beyond. All multiples of 5 end in 0 or 5.

Counting in fives from other numbers

When counting on or back in fives starting on other numbers you can also see patterns in the unit digits.

Counting on in fives from 2

2, 7, 12, 17, 22, 27, 32, 37 ...
(The unit digits are 2 or 7)

Counting back in fives from 94

94, 89, 84, 79, 74, 69, 64, 59 ...
(The unit digits are 4 or 9)

Now it's your turn. Count on in fives from 1 and see where the numbers are on the 100 square.

1, 6, 11, 16, 21, 26 ...
(The unit digits are 1 or 6)

1	2	3	4	5	6	7	8	9	10
11	12	13	14	15	16	17	18	19	20
21	22	23	24	25	26	27	28	29	30
31	32	33	34	35	36	37	38	39	40
41	42	43	44	45	46	47	48	49	50
51	52	53	54	55	56	57	58	59	60
61	62	63	64	65	66	67	68	69	70
71	72	73	74	75	76	77	78	79	80
81	82	83	84	85	86	87	88	89	90
91	92	93	94	95	96	97	98	99	100

Test yourself!

1 Count on in fives from 36 to 96.

2 Count back in fives from 53 to 3.

3 Find the next three numbers in these patterns.
   a) 38, 43, 48, 53, ..., ..., ...,
   b) 95, 90, 85, 80, ..., ..., ...,
   c) 47, 52, 57, 62, ..., ..., ...,

(For more about multiples, see page 27.)

Remember

When you count on or back in fives, every other unit digit is the same.

Number patterns

Finding missing numbers

When we **count on in equal steps** we make a **pattern** or sequence.
In the example below there is a pattern, but one number is missing.

Find the missing number in this pattern:

- Decide whether the pattern is going up or down.

- Decide whether the pattern is going in 1s, 2s, 5s or 10s or other sized steps.

- This pattern is going up in 2s.

- The missing number must be 2 more than 8.

Answer: 10

Find the missing number in this pattern:

- This pattern is going down in 10s, so the missing number must be 10 less than 63, and 10 more than 43.

Answer: 53

Find the missing two numbers in this pattern:

This pattern is going up in 5s, so the missing numbers must be:

- 5 more than 17, which is **22**

- 5 more than 27, which is **32**

Answer: 22   32

Test yourself!

I   Find the missing numbers in these patterns:

a) 3, 5, 7, ..., 11, 13

b) 2, 12, 22, ..., ..., 52

c) 67, 65, ..., 61, ..., 57

d) 8, 13, ..., 23, 28, ...

Remember

Decide whether the pattern is going **up** or **down**.

Decide whether it is going in **1s, 2s, 5s** or **10s**, or other sized steps.

Estimating

To estimate means to make a 'good guess'.

Estimate the number of lemons

Don't count them!
How many do you think there are?
Make a good guess.

Do you think there are more than 20?

Do you think there are more than 10 or less than 10?

Useful tip

It sometimes helps to see the things as groups, like this:

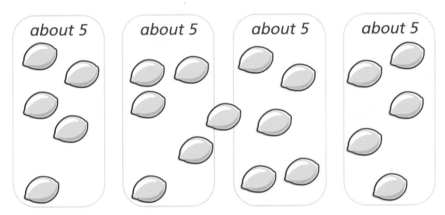

about 5   about 5   about 5   about 5

Then you can say that there are about 20.
Your guess does not have to be exactly right!

Remember

Don't count – just make a good guess. Group the things if it helps.

Test yourself!

1 Estimate the number of mushrooms below.

2 Estimate the number of peppers below.

Ordering

Ordering numbers to 100

When ordering numbers, make sure you know what **each digit** in the number stands for, like **tens** and **units**.

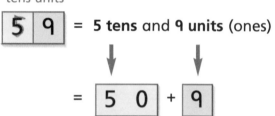

tens units

| 5 | 9 | = 5 tens and 9 units (ones)

= 5 0 + 9

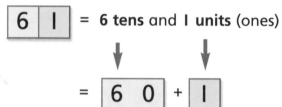

tens units

| 6 | 1 | = 6 tens and 1 units (ones)

= 6 0 + 1

Which number is larger, 59 or 61?

61 has **6 tens** and 59 has only **5 tens**, so 61 is **larger** than 59.

Answer: 61

Put these numbers in order, starting with the smallest:

58,   71,   19,   42,   80

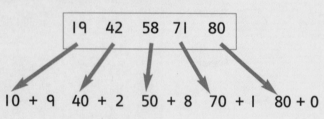

19   42   58   71   80

10 + 9   40 + 2   50 + 8   70 + 1   80 + 0

Answer: 19, 42, 58, 71, 80

Remember

When ordering numbers, make sure you know what **each digit** in the number stands for.

Test yourself!

1 Order these numbers, starting with the smallest:
a) 52, 64, 73, 13, 39
b) 47, 69, 42, 79, 21
c) 90, 57, 81, 18, 80

2 How many tens has each of these numbers?
a) 59
b) 32
c) 95

3 Split these numbers into parts (the first one has been done for you):
a) 46 = 40 + 6
b) 84 =
c) 93 =
d) 37 =

Ordering

Ordering numbers to 1000

When ordering numbers, make sure you know what **each digit** in the number stands for, like **hundreds, tens** and **units**.

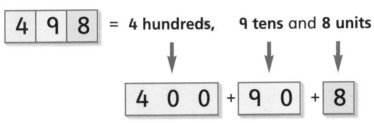

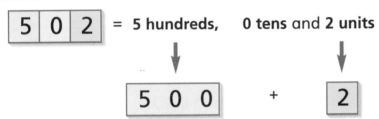

Which number is larger, 498 or 502?

502 has **5 hundreds** and 498 only has **4 hundreds**, so 502 is **larger** than 498.

Answer: **502**

Put these numbers in order, starting with the smallest:

490,   362,   500,   946,   601

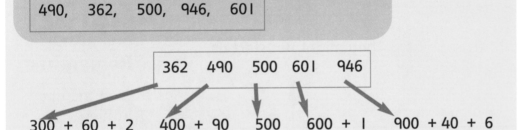

Remember

When ordering numbers, make sure you know what **each digit** in the number stands for – **hundreds, tens** or **units**.

Test yourself!

1 Order these numbers, starting with the smallest:
   a) 572, 644, 743, 193, 379
   b) 487, 629, 411, 709, 251

2 How many hundreds has each of these numbers?
   a) 589
   b) 732
   c) 295

3 Split these numbers into parts (the first one has been done for you):
   a) 146 = 100 + 40 + 6
   b) 439 =
   c) 721 =
   d) 297 =

Number lines

Estimating numbers on number lines

Numbers can be arranged on **number lines**, like these:

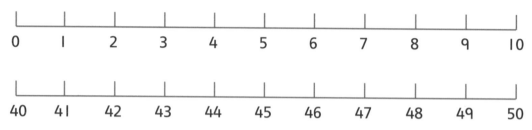

Sometimes not all the numbers are marked, like this:

You have to work out what number the arrow is pointing to.

Estimate the number the arrow is pointing to

To make a good estimate, split the line into equal parts and mark on other numbers.

About 75

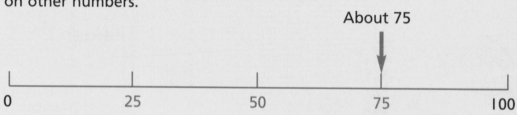

Always look carefully at the numbers. They might **not** start at **zero**.

In the example above, the arrow is pointing to about 35.

Remember

Split the line into equal parts to help you make a good estimate.

Test yourself!

1 Look at the number lines below. Estimate the numbers that the arrows are pointing to.

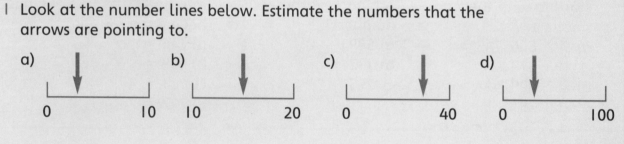

a)   b)   c)   d)

Fractions

A fraction is part of something that has been split into equal parts.
There are many different fractions.

Halves

A half is **one out of two equal pieces** and is written $\frac{1}{2}$.
These have all been split into halves.

Quarters

A quarter is **one out of four equal pieces** and is written $\frac{1}{4}$.
These have all been split into quarters.

Three quarters is **three out of four equal pieces** and is
written $\frac{3}{4}$.

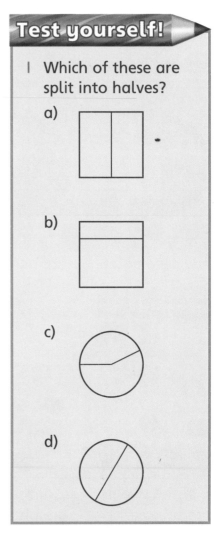

Test yourself!

I Which of these are split into halves?

a)

b)

c)

d)

Remember

Fractions are **equal** parts of things.

Fractions

Finding fractions

What fraction of these shapes is red?

 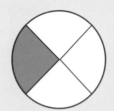 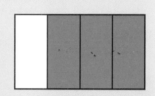

I out of 2 equal parts is red so $\frac{1}{2}$ is red.

I out of 4 equal parts is red so $\frac{1}{4}$ is red.

3 out of 4 equal parts are red so $\frac{3}{4}$ is red.

What fraction of the cake has been eaten?

$\frac{1}{2}$ of the cake has been eaten.

$\frac{1}{4}$ of the cake has been eaten.

$\frac{3}{4}$ of the cake has been eaten.

What fraction of the sweets are blue?

$\frac{1}{2}$ of the sweets are blue.

$\frac{1}{4}$ of the sweets are blue.

$\frac{3}{4}$ of the sweets are blue.

Test yourself!

I What fraction of these shapes is red?

a)

b)

2 What fraction of the pencils is blue?

a)

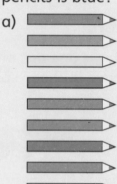

b)

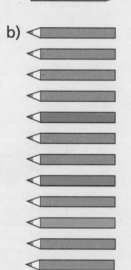

Remember

One out of **two equal parts** is $\frac{1}{2}$.   **One** out of **four equal parts** is $\frac{1}{4}$.

Fractions

Fractions that are equal

One half of this square is red.

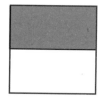

Two quarters of this square are red.

One half of these sweets are ringed.

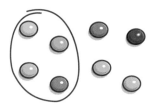

Two quarters of these sweets are ringed.

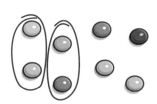

Can you see that **one half** $\frac{1}{2}$ and **two quarters** $\frac{2}{4}$ are the same?

Fractions on a number line

We can mark a fraction on a number line.

Mark $3\frac{1}{2}$ on this number line

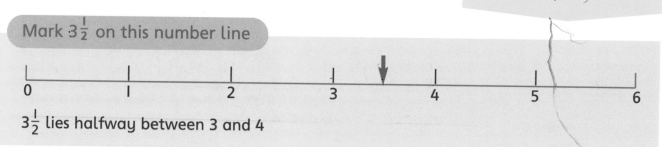

$3\frac{1}{2}$ lies halfway between 3 and 4

Mark $7\frac{1}{2}$ on this number line

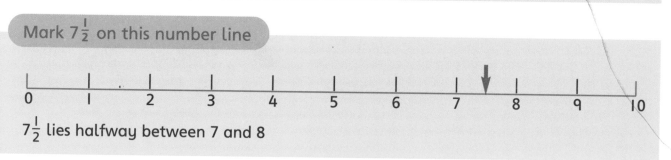

$7\frac{1}{2}$ lies halfway between 7 and 8

Remember

One half $\frac{1}{2}$ and **two quarters** $\frac{2}{4}$ are the same.

Mental addition

Addition words

These are all words that can mean addition:

more   add   plus   total
altogether   sum   and

We use this sign + to mean add. We write 12 + 7 = 19

Splitting numbers up to add them

We can split numbers like 26 into 20 and 6. This can make it easier to add numbers.

Split 37 into tens and units

3 7

30 + 7

Add 26 and 13

First, split up the numbers.

2 6 + 1 3

20 + 6   10 + 3

Then add the tens.   20 + 10 = 30

Next add the units.   6 + 3 = 9

Then we add the total tens   30 + 9 = 39
and the total units.

Answer: **39**

Test yourself!

1 Split these numbers
   into tens and units:
   a) 29
   b) 46
   c) 78

2 Add these numbers:
   a) 27 + 12
   b) 16 + 25
   c) 26 + 37

Remember

We can **split numbers** (like 49) into **tens and units** (40 and 9). This makes addition easier.

Mental addition

Adding 10

When **adding 10** just add 1 to the **tens** column.

39 + 10 = 49

75 + 10 = 85

Adding 100

When **adding 100** just add 1 to the **hundreds** column.

247 + 100 = 347

582 + 100 = 682

Adding three numbers

There are two different ways of adding three numbers.

Find pairs that add to 10 and add these first

Add 3 + 5 + 7

Look at 3 + 5 + 7

You know that 3 + 7 = 10

So just do 3 + 7 + 5 = 15   It's easier!

Start with the largest number first

Add 4 + 8 + 3

Look at 4 + 8 + 3

8 is the biggest.
4 is the next biggest.

So just do 8 + 4 + 3 = 15   It's easier!

Test yourself!

1 Add 10 to these numbers:
 a) 43
 b) 58
 c) 89

2 Add 100 to these numbers:
 a) 145
 b) 387
 c) 802

3 Add these numbers:
 a) 5 + 6 + 4
 b) 1 + 8 + 9
 c) 6 + 7 + 9

Remember

When adding three numbers you can **change the order** to make it easier.

Always look for **pairs that add to 10**.

Mental addition

Doubles

Learn these doubles:

1 + 1 = 2	6 + 6 = 12	11 + 11 = 22
2 + 2 = 4	7 + 7 = 14	12 + 12 = 24
3 + 3 = 6	8 + 8 = 16	13 + 13 = 26
4 + 4 = 8	9 + 9 = 18	14 + 14 = 28
5 + 5 = 10	10 + 10 = 20	15 + 15 = 30
20 + 20 = 40	25 + 25 = 50	30 + 30 = 60
35 + 35 = 70	40 + 40 = 80	45 + 45 = 90

and finally, don't forget: **50 + 50 = 100**

Using 'near doubles'

When we add numbers that are '**next to each other**', like 6 and 7, 9 and 10 or 15 and 16, we can: **double one of the numbers and then add or subtract one.**

6 + 7

6 + 6 + 1 = 13   or   7 + 7 − 1 = 13

9 + 10

10 + 10 − 1 = 19

15 + 16

15 + 15 + 1 = 31

The rule is:

- If you doubled the **higher** number, **subtract** one.
- If you doubled the **lower** number, **add** one.

Test yourself!

1 Cover the doubles table on the left and answer these:
   a) 13 + 13
   b) 11 + 11
   c) 35 + 35

2 Add these numbers:
   a) 9 + 8
   b) 10 + 11
   c) 12 + 13
   d) 14 + 15
   e) 19 + 20

Did you know?

To add **30 + 30**, remember that
3 + 3 = 6,
so **30 + 30 = 60**

For more on doubles, see page 30.

Remember

After you have doubled one of the numbers, think carefully about whether to **add** or **subtract** one.

Mental addition

Adding numbers close to 10, 20, 30 etc.

When we are adding numbers like 9, 19, 29, ... and so on, we can just add 10, 20 or 30 and then subtract 1. See how this works on the number lines below.

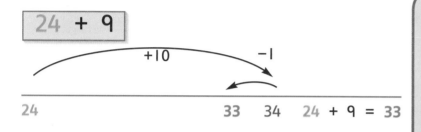

$24 + 9 = 33$

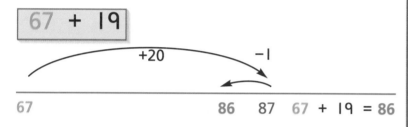

$67 + 19 = 86$

We can even do it with numbers like 18, 28, 38 etc. You must remember to subtract 2 this time, because the numbers are 2 less than 20, 30, 40 etc.

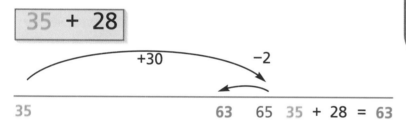

$35 + 28 = 63$

Using addition patterns

We can use easy addition to help with harder addition.

Write a sum you know: $3 + 5 = 8$ or $4 + 7 = 11$

Watch what happens when you add 10 to one of the numbers. Look at the patterns:

We can use this pattern to see that:

$3 + 5 = 8$	$4 + 7 = 11$
$13 + 5 = 18$	$4 + 17 = 21$
$23 + 5 = 28$	$4 + 27 = 31$
$33 + 5 = 38$	$4 + 37 = 41$

Did you know?

When you are adding 11, you can: **add 10 and then add 1**

$$35 + 11$$

is the same as

$$35 + 10 + 1 = 46$$

When you are adding 21, you can: **add 20 and then add 1**

$$35 + 21$$

is the same as

$$35 + 20 + 1 = 56$$

Now you can work out how to add 31, 41, 51, etc.!

Test yourself!

1 Add these numbers:
  a) $26 + 9$
  b) $58 + 19$
  c) $47 + 29$
  d) $36 + 18$
  e) $74 + 38$

Remember

To add numbers like 9, 19, 29 ... or 18, 28, 38 and so on ... add 10, 20 or 30 and then subtract 1 or 2.

Mental subtraction

Subtraction words

These are all words that can mean subtraction:

minus

subtract

less than

fewer

take away

difference between

The subtraction sign

We use this sign − to mean subtract.
We write 12 − 7 = 5

Splitting numbers up

We can split numbers like 53 into 50 and 3.
This can make it easier to subtract numbers.

Split 53 into tens and units

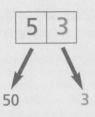

| 5 | 3 |

50   3

35 subtract 18

| 3 | 5 | − | 1 | 8 |

10   8

35 − 10 = 25

25 − 8 = 17

Answer: **17**

Test yourself!

1 Which of these are addition words and which are subtraction?
   a) more
   b) total
   c) less than
   d) minus
   e) fewer
   f) altogether

2 Subtract these numbers:
   a) 54 − 13
   b) 65 − 24
   c) 73 − 27

Remember

We can split numbers like 18 into 10 and 8 to make subtraction easier.

Mental subtraction

Subtracting 10

When subtracting **10**, just take **1** from the **tens** column.

    48 – 10 = 38
    67 – 10 = 57

Subtracting 100

When subtracting **100**, just take **1** from the **hundreds** column.

    537 – 100 = 437
    946 – 100 = 846

Finding differences by counting on

We can find the difference between numbers by counting on.

> Find the difference between 78 and 83

Count on from 78 to 83   78 79 80 81 82 83

Answer: **The difference between 78 and 83 is 5**

Another method is to use a blank number line.

> Find the difference between 78 and 83

Use a blank number line with 80 as a 'stepping stone':

2 + 3 = 5

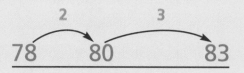

Remember

We can find the **difference** between numbers by **counting on**.

Test yourself!

1 Subtract 10 from these numbers:
   a) 67
   b) 76
   c) 89

2 Subtract 100 from these numbers:
   a) 375
   b) 603
   c) 999

3 Find the difference between:
   a) 58 and 63
   b) 47 and 54
   c) 65 and 72
   d) 84 and 93

Mental subtraction

Subtracting numbers close to 10, 20, 30 etc.

When we are subtracting numbers like 9, 19, 29, ... and so on, we can just subtract 10, 20 or 30 and then add 1. See how this works on the number lines below.

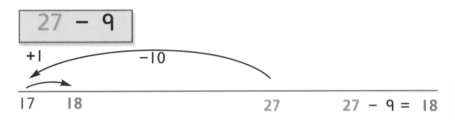

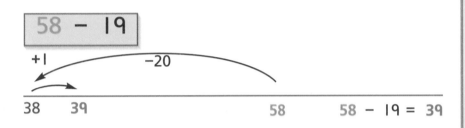

We can even do it with numbers like 18, 28, 38 etc. You must remember to **add** 2 this time, because the numbers are **2 less** than 20, 30, 40 etc.

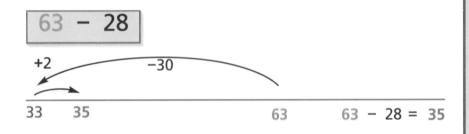

Using subtraction patterns

We can use easy subtraction to help us with harder subtraction. Write a subtraction you know:

$$5 - 4 = 1 \quad \text{or} \quad 9 - 6 = 3$$

Watch what happens when you add 10 to one of the numbers. Look at the patterns:

5 − 4 = 1	9 − 6 = 3
15 − 4 = 11	19 − 6 = 13
25 − 4 = 21	29 − 6 = 23
35 − 4 = 31	39 − 6 = 33

We can use this pattern to see that:

Did you know?

When you are subtracting numbers like 11, 21, 31 etc. You can subtract 10 and then subtract another 1, or subtract 20 and then subtract 1:

54 − 21

54 − 20 − 1 = 33

Remember

To subtract numbers like 9, 19, 29 ... or 18, 28, 38 and so on ... subtract **10, 20** or **30** and then **add 1** or **2**.

Addition and subtraction facts

Partners to 10

You need to know all the pairs of numbers that **total 10**:

0 + 10 = 10	3 + 7 = 10	5 + 5 = 10	7 + 3 = 10	9 + 1 = 10
1 + 9 = 10	4 + 6 = 10	6 + 4 = 10	8 + 2 = 10	10 + 0 = 10
2 + 8 = 10				

Partners to 20

You need to know all the pairs of numbers that **total 20**:

0 + 20 = 20	5 + 15 = 20	9 + 11 = 20	13 + 7 = 20	17 + 3 = 20
1 + 19 = 20	6 + 14 = 20	10 + 10 = 20	14 + 6 = 20	18 + 2 = 20
2 + 18 = 20	7 + 13 = 20	11 + 9 = 20	15 + 5 = 20	19 + 1 = 20
3 + 17 = 20	8 + 12 = 20	12 + 8 = 20	16 + 4 = 20	20 + 0 = 20
4 + 16 = 20				

Partners to 100

You should know these pairs of numbers that **total 100**:

10 + 90 = 100	40 + 60 = 100	70 + 30 = 100
20 + 80 = 100	50 + 50 = 100	80 + 20 = 100
30 + 70 = 100	60 + 40 = 100	90 + 10 = 100

If you know an addition fact then you also know some subtraction facts:

11 + 9 = 20

so you also know

20 − 11 = 9 and 20 − 9 = 11

Remember

Knowing partners to **10, 20** and **100** will help you to work in your head more easily.

If you know an **addition** fact then you also know some **subtraction** facts.

Test yourself!

1 Cover the partners to 10.
Answer these:
a) ... + 4 = 10
b) 9 + ... = 10
c) ... + 8 = 10
d) 3 + ... = 10

2 Cover the partners to 20.
Answer these:
a) 11 + ... = 20
b) ... + 4 = 20
c) 13 + ... = 20
d) ... + 12 = 20

3 Cover the partners to 100.
Answer these:
a) 80 + ... = 100
b) ... + 40 = 100
c) 30 + ... = 100

Multiplication

Multiplication is a quick way of adding **the same number many times**. We multiply or 'times' one number by another. Look at this:

These tins of beans come in packs of three.
I have four packs of tins.
How many tins are there?

3   +   3   +   3   +   3

Multiplication helps us to add more quickly.

This can be written as four **times** three   or   four **multiplied by** three

4 lots of 3   or   4 × 3

If you know the tables fact $\boxed{4 \times 3 = 12}$ then you don't need to add!

The answer is **12 tins**.

Here are 8 five pence coins.
How much money is there?

5 + 5 + 5 + 5 + 5 + 5 + 5 + 5

This can be written as

8 lots of 5   or   8 × 5

If you know the tables fact $\boxed{8 \times 5 = 40}$

then you don't need to add! The answer is **40p**.

Test yourself!

1   Write these questions as multiplication questions (the first one has been done for you):
   a) 2 + 2 + 2 + 2 = 4 x 2
   b) 5 + 5 + 5 + 5 =
   c) 3 + 3 + 3 + 3 + 3 =
   d) 4 + 4 + 4 =
   e) 10 + 10 + 10 + 10 =
   f) 3 + 3 + 3 + 3 =
   g) 5 + 5 + 5 =
   h) 2 + 2 + 2 + 2 + 2 =

Remember

Learn your **tables facts** (see next page) to save you from having to add many times.

Tables facts

Look at these **tables facts**. Learn as many of these facts as you can.

Table of 2s	Table of 3s	Table of 4s	Table of 5s	Table of 10s
1 × 2 = 2	1 × 3 = 3	1 × 4 = 4	1 × 5 = 5	1 × 10 = 10
2 × 2 = 4	2 × 3 = 6	2 × 4 = 8	2 × 5 = 10	2 × 10 = 20
3 × 2 = 6	3 × 3 = 9	3 × 4 = 12	3 × 5 = 15	3 × 10 = 30
4 × 2 = 8	4 × 3 = 12	4 × 4 = 16	4 × 5 = 20	4 × 10 = 40
5 × 2 = 10	5 × 3 = 15	5 × 4 = 20	5 × 5 = 25	5 × 10 = 50
6 × 2 = 12	6 × 3 = 18	6 × 4 = 24	6 × 5 = 30	6 × 10 = 60
7 × 2 = 14	7 × 3 = 21	7 × 4 = 28	7 × 5 = 35	7 × 10 = 70
8 × 2 = 16	8 × 3 = 24	8 × 4 = 32	8 × 5 = 40	8 × 10 = 80
9 × 2 = 18	9 × 3 = 27	9 × 4 = 36	9 × 5 = 45	9 × 10 = 90
10 × 2 = 20	10 × 3 = 30	10 × 4 = 40	10 × 5 = 50	10 × 10 = 100

5 × 2 = 10

Look at the two facts in red.

Notice that 5 × 2 has the same answer as 2 × 5

10 × 3 = 30

Look at the two facts in green.

Notice that 10 × 3 has the same answer as 3 × 10

Test yourself!

1 Cover the page and see how many of these answers you know:

2 × 3	3 × 5
5 × 10	4 × 2
6 × 3	7 × 10
8 × 2	6 × 5
9 × 4	7 × 3
6 × 10	5 × 4
3 × 3	8 × 5

Switching around the numbers

The numbers in **any** tables fact can be switched around and the answer will be the same. Look at the examples below.

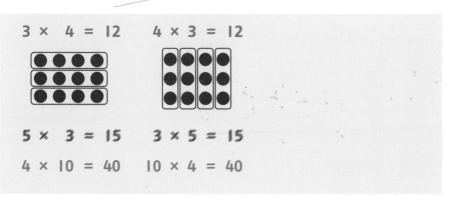

3 × 4 = 12   4 × 3 = 12

5 × 3 = 15   3 × 5 = 15

4 × 10 = 40   10 × 4 = 40

This means that for every fact you learn, you also learn another fact!

Multiples

A **tables fact answer** is always called a multiple. For example, 40 is a multiple of 4 **and** a multiple of 10 because it is in **both** tables.

Remember

The numbers in **any** tables fact can be switched round and the answer will be the same.

Division

Division is about **sharing** or sorting things into **groups**.

Sharing

6 ÷ 2 (6 divided by 2) can be thought of as 6 shared between 2.

Share six bears between two people

Each person gets **3**

so   6 ÷ 2 = **3**

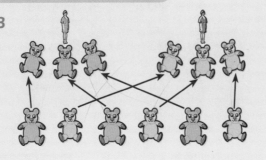

Grouping

6 ÷ 2 (6 divided by 2) can also be thought of as 6 grouped into 2s.

Sort these six people into groups of twos

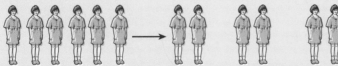

There are **3** groups altogether

so   6 ÷ 2 = **3**

You can use either **sharing** or **grouping** to find the answer to division questions like the one below.

Find the answer to 8 ÷ 2

Sharing	**Grouping**
Share out 8 sweets between 2 people.	Group 8 sweets into groups of 2.
How many do they get each?	How many groups are there?
Answer: **4**	Answer: **4**

Test yourself!

1 Answer these division questions using sharing:
   a) 4 ÷ 2
   b) 6 ÷ 3
   c) 12 ÷ 4
   d) 15 ÷ 5

2 Answer these division questions using grouping:
   a) 10 ÷ 2
   b) 9 ÷ 3
   c) 12 ÷ 3
   d) 20 ÷ 5

For larger numbers it is often easier to use grouping.

Remember

You can use either sharing or grouping to work out division answers.

Division facts

Doing **division** is much easier if you learn division facts.
Division facts are like tables facts, but the other way round.

Look at these tables facts:

$3 \times 4 = 12$ and $4 \times 3 = 12$

These division facts are also related:

$12 \div 3 = 4$ and $12 \div 4 = 3$

÷ 2	÷ 3	÷ 4	÷ 5	÷ 10
$2 \div 2 = 1$	$3 \div 3 = 1$	$4 \div 4 = 1$	$5 \div 5 = 1$	$10 \div 10 = 1$
$4 \div 2 = 2$	$6 \div 3 = 2$	$8 \div 4 = 2$	$10 \div 5 = 2$	$20 \div 10 = 2$
$6 \div 2 = 3$	$9 \div 3 = 3$	$12 \div 4 = 3$	$15 \div 5 = 3$	$30 \div 10 = 3$
$8 \div 2 = 4$	$12 \div 3 = 4$	$16 \div 4 = 4$	$20 \div 5 = 4$	$40 \div 10 = 4$
$10 \div 2 = 5$	$15 \div 3 = 5$	$20 \div 4 = 5$	$25 \div 5 = 5$	$50 \div 10 = 5$
$12 \div 2 = 6$	$18 \div 3 = 6$	$24 \div 4 = 6$	$30 \div 5 = 6$	$60 \div 10 = 6$
$14 \div 2 = 7$	$21 \div 3 = 7$	$28 \div 4 = 7$	$35 \div 5 = 7$	$70 \div 10 = 7$
$16 \div 2 = 8$	$24 \div 3 = 8$	$32 \div 4 = 8$	$40 \div 5 = 8$	$80 \div 10 = 8$
$18 \div 2 = 9$	$27 \div 3 = 9$	$36 \div 4 = 9$	$45 \div 5 = 9$	$90 \div 10 = 9$
$20 \div 2 = 10$	$30 \div 3 = 10$	$40 \div 4 = 10$	$50 \div 5 = 10$	$100 \div 10 = 10$

Switching around the numbers

The numbers in division facts can be switched around,
like these. Look at the examples below.

$15 \div 3 = 5$ $15 \div 5 = 3$

$40 \div 10 = 4$ $40 \div 4 = 10$

This means that for every fact you learn, you also learn another fact!

Test yourself!

1 Cover the page and see how many of these answers you know:

$6 \div 3$	$15 \div 5$
$50 \div 10$	$8 \div 2$
$18 \div 3$	$70 \div 10$
$16 \div 2$	$30 \div 5$
$36 \div 4$	$21 \div 3$
$60 \div 10$	$20 \div 4$
$9 \div 3$	$40 \div 5$

Remember

Use **facts that you already know**, like **tables facts** or other **division facts**.

Doubling and halving

Doubling

Use **doubling** when multiplying by 2 or adding two of the same number together.

> **5 + 5**
>
> 5 + 5 can be thought of as
>
> 2 × 5,   5 × 2,   double 5   or   twice 5

Once you know doubles by heart you can use them to answer 'near-doubles' questions. Find out more about this and the doubles you should know on page 20.

Halving

Use halving when dividing by 2.

> **10 ÷ 2**
>
> 10 ÷ 2 can be thought of as
>
> half of 10   or $\frac{1}{2}$ of 10

Learn these halves

half of 2 = 1	half of 4 = 2	half of 6 = 3
half of 8 = 4	half of 10 = 5	half of 12 = 6
half of 14 = 7	half of 16 = 8	half of 18 = 9
half of 20 = 10	half of 30 = 15	half of 40 = 20
half of 50 = 25	half of 60 = 30	half of 70 = 35
half of 80 = 40	half of 90 = 45	half of 100 = 50

Notice that **halving facts** are related to **doubling facts**.

double 7 = 14   half of 14 = 7
15 + 15 = 30   half of 30 = 15

Test yourself!

1 Double these numbers:
a) 8
b) 12
c) 6
d) 14
e) 9
f) 7
g) 13
h) 35

2 Halve these numbers:
a) 22
b) 16
c) 50
d) 18
e) 70
f) 40
g) 90
h) 100

Remember

Once you know a **double**, you can **switch it around** to make a **halving fact**.

25 + 25 = 50 so
half of 50 = 25

Number stories

Do you add, subtract, multiply or divide?

Look at this number story:

A cat has four legs. Five cats have 20 legs altogether.

This number story can be written as the number statement: **5 × 4 = 20**

Here are some other number stories and the statements that go with them:

A woman has four cats, her sister has five cats. They have nine cats altogether.

Number statement: **4 + 5 = 9**

A man has eight cat chews. He shares them between his two cats. Each cat gets four chews.

Number statement: **8 ÷ 2 = 4**

A tin of cat food cost 35p. Mrs Wood paid with a 50p coin. She was given 15p change.

Number statement: **50 − 35 = 15**

Making up your own number stories

Practise making up your own number stories to match these statements. You could think about stories with sweets, fruit, animals or money.

12 − 8 = 4   15 + 15 = 30

14 ÷ 2 = 7   5 × 3 = 15

Test yourself!

1   Write the number statements for these stories.
   a) James had 35p. He was given another 17p. He now has 52p.
   b) A person has two legs. Seven people have 14 legs.
   c) I had 16 sweets. I ate nine of them. I have seven left.
   d) 20 children got into groups of two. There were 10 groups.

Remember

Write number statements and practise making up your own number stories.

Number problems

Solving problems

The word 'solve' means 'find the answer to'.

To solve a number problem, first decide whether to add, subtract, multiply or divide.

A dog has four legs.
How many legs have three dogs?

This can be written as $3 \times 4 = ?$

Now work out the answer. Here we could add three lots of four or use tables facts.

Answer: 12 legs

$$\begin{array}{r} 4 \\ 4 \\ + \ 4 \\ \hline 12 \end{array} \qquad 3 \times 4 = 12$$

A tin of dog food cost 37p. Mrs Wood paid with a 50p coin. How much change was she given?

This can be written as $50 - 37 = ?$

Now work out the answer. Here we could count on from 37 up to 50 or subtract 37 from 50.

| +10p | + 3p |
37p   47p   50p $50 - 37 = 13p$

Answer: 13p

(See page 35 for more on finding change.)

Test yourself!

1 Answer these questions:

a) Ravi had 45p. He was given another 27p. How much has he now?

b) A person has two legs. How many legs have eight people?

c) I had 24 sweets. I ate nine of them. How many have I now?

d) 18 children got into groups of two. How many groups are there?

Remember

To solve a number problem, first decide whether to add, subtract, multiply or divide.

Number problems

More than one answer

Some number problems and puzzles have more than one correct answer. As long as the answer you give is correct, it doesn't matter if someone else gives a different answer.

Look at the puzzle below.

Use some of these cards to make a correct number statement:

You could give any of the following answers:

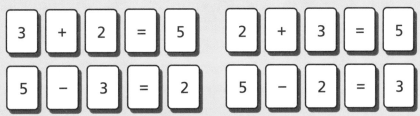

You could even put the equals sign here

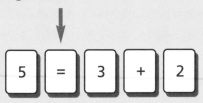

What is on one side of the equals sign is worth the same as what is on the other side, so it is correct.

Write two numbers with a sum of 12

'Sum' means 'total' or numbers added together.

Here are some correct answers:

11 and 1,   10 and 2,   9 and 3,   8 and 4,   7 and 5, ...

Remember

Don't worry if there is more than one answer.

Make sure the answer you give is correct.

Test yourself!

1 Answer these questions:
   a) Write two numbers with a sum of 15
   b) Write two numbers with a difference of 3

2 Use some of these cards to make a correct number statement:

   a)

   b) | 6 | 2 | 3 | 1 | = | × | ÷ |

Money

Coins in Great Britain

Make sure you know what each of these coins is worth.

Paying exactly

Different coins can be used to **pay exactly** (without needing change).

You can buy this toy

using these coins

or these coins

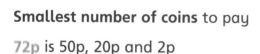

Using the smallest number of coins

To find the **smallest number of coins** to pay for something costing 72p:

- Pick the largest coin **less** than the amount   72p

- See how much more is left to pay.   72p − 50p = 22p

- Pick the largest coin **less** than this amount   22p

- See how much more is left to pay.

  22p − 20p = 2p

Smallest number of coins to pay

72p is 50p, 20p and 2p

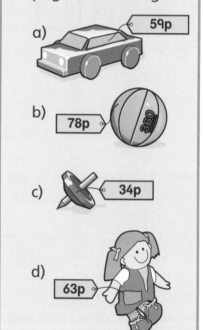

Test yourself!

1 Find the totals of these coins:
  a) 10p and 5p
  b) 2p, 2p, 5p and 1p
  c) 10p, 20p
  d) 20p, 50p
  e) 20p, 5p, 2p
  f) £1, £2
  g) 50p, 10p, 5p, 1p

2 Find the smallest number of coins to pay for these toys:

  a)   59p

  b)   78p

  c)   34p

  d)   63p

Remember

To find the smallest number of coins to pay for something exactly, always start with the largest coin you can use.

Money

Finding how much change you will be given

Sometimes you don't have the exact money to pay for something. You might pay with a larger coin and be given change. Here are two ways to find out how much change you will be given.

1. **Count on** from the price until you get to the coin amount.

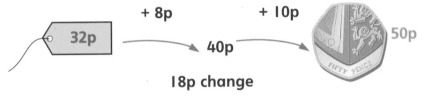

+ 8p   + 10p

32p → 40p → 50p

18p change

2. **Take away** the price from the coin you gave.

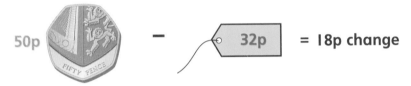

50p − 32p = 18p change

Find how much change you will get

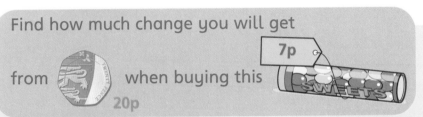

from   20p   when buying this   7p   SWEETS

1. **Count on**

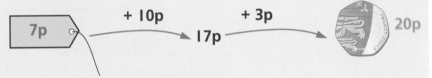

+ 10p   + 3p

7p → 17p → 20p

Answer: 13p

or

2. **Take away**

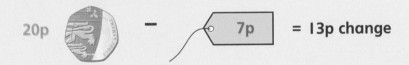

20p − 7p = 13p change

Answer: 13p

Remember

To find change, either:
- **count on** from the price to the coin amount
- or **take away** the price from the coin amount.

Length

Finding out how long something is

To find out how long something is we measure its length.
We can measure **length** in **centimetres** and **metres**.

centimetres	metres
short things, like pencils, hands, feet	long things, like the floor, playground, hall

There are 100 centimetres (cm) in a metre (m).

We can measure length with a ruler, tape measure, trundle wheel or metre stick.

Using a ruler

We use a ruler to measure these lines in centimetres, like this:

_____ 8cm

cm	1	2	3	4	5	6	7	8	9	10

_____ 10cm

Always line up your ruler on the end of the line.

Estimating

You might be asked to estimate the length of a wiggly line.

How long do you think this wiggly worm is?

Try to imagine the wiggly worm pulled straight.
You could also use string to lie along the line.
Then pull it straight and measure with a ruler.

Answer: About 12cm.

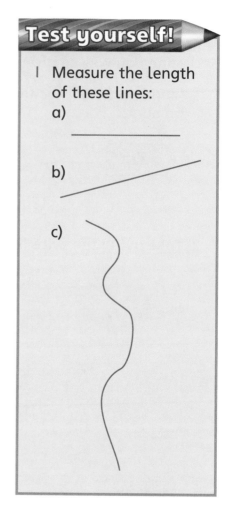

Did you know?

We can shorten the word **centimetre** to **cm** and **metre** to **m**.

Remember

Always **line up** your ruler on the **end of the line**.

There are **100 centimetres** (cm) in a **metre** (m).

Mass

Finding out how heavy something is

To find out how heavy something is we measure its
mass. Mass is sometimes called **weight**. We measure
mass in **grams** and **kilograms**.

grams
light things,
like eggs,
socks, books

kilograms
heavy things,
like people,
bags of sugar

There are 1000 grams (g) in a kilogram (kg).

Using measuring scales

We can measure mass with measuring scales, like these

bathroom scales

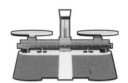

balance scales

kitchen scales

How heavy are these parcels?

A

B

Answer: Parcel A weighs $3\frac{1}{2}$ kg and
Parcel B weighs 750g

Estimating

Look at some objects around you, such as a book, a bag
of potatoes – even yourself! Have a guess at their mass.
Then weigh them to find out if your guesses were right!

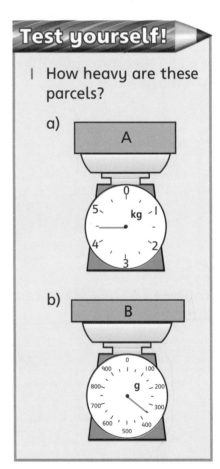

Test yourself!

I How heavy are these
    parcels?

a)

A

b)

B

Did you know?

We can shorten the
word **gram** to **g** and
kilogram to **kg**.

Remember

There are **1000 grams**
(g) in a **kilogram** (kg).

Capacity

Finding out how much something holds

To find out how much something holds we measure its capacity. We measure **capacity** in **millilitres** and **litres**.

millilitres	litres
how much a cup or mug will hold	how much a bucket or bowl will hold

There are 1000 millilitres (ml) in a litre (l).

We can measure capacity using jugs and containers like these:

You need to be able to read scales on containers like these.

How much juice is in each container?

A   B   C

Answers: A: 500ml, B: 300ml, C: 850ml

Estimating

Look at some containers around you, such as a cup, a bottle of lemonade and a sink. Have a guess at their capacity. Then find out whether your guesses were correct!

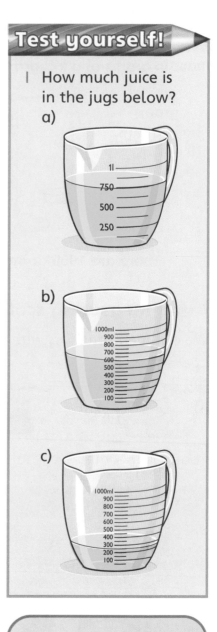

Did you know?

We can shorten the word **millilitre** to **ml** and **litre** to **l**.

Remember

There are **1000 millilitres** (ml) in a **litre** (l).

Time

The **little hand** on a clock or watch shows the hour.

The **big hand** shows the minutes.

two o'clock

Halves and quarters

quarter past two

We call this 'quarter past' because the **big hand** has gone round one quarter of the clock

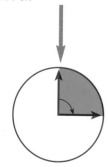

half past two

We call this 'half past' because the **big hand** has gone round one half of the clock

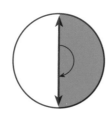

quarter to three

We call this 'quarter to' because the **big hand** has gone round three quarters of the clock and it has one quarter to go

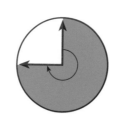

Test yourself!

1 What time does each clock show?

a)

b)

c)

Did you know?

60 seconds = 1 minute
60 minutes = 1 hour
24 hours = 1 day
7 days = 1 week
52 weeks = 1 year

Remember

The **little hand** on a clock or watch shows the **hour.**

The **big hand** shows the **minutes.**

Time

Telling the time

The number the little hand is nearest to shows the hour.

The hour hand is just past two. The time is quarter past two

The hour hand is nearly at five. The time is quarter to five

The big hand shows how many minutes to or past the hour.

It's ten minutes past five

It's twenty minutes to seven

Between two numbers there are 5 minutes

Can you tell the time on these clocks?

1

2

3

It's twenty-five minutes past seven

It's five minutes to nine

It's twenty-five to four

Sometimes we miss out the word 'minutes'

Days

Learn the names of the days in order:

- Sunday
- Monday
- Tuesday
- Wednesday
- Thursday
- Friday
- Saturday

Months

Learn the names of the months in order:

January	July
February	August
March	September
April	October
May	November
June	December

1 What time do these clocks show?

a)

b)

c)

d)

2 a) Which day follows Tuesday?
   b) Which day follows Saturday?

3 a) Which month comes after March?
   b) Which month comes before August?

Remember

The number the little hand is nearest to shows the hour.

The big hand shows how many minutes to or past the hour.

Time

Digital clocks

Digital clocks don't have hands. They just have numbers. Tell the time by saying one number after the other, like this.

Five thirty

Eight forty-five

Matching digital and ordinary clocks

Digital and ordinary clocks show the time in different ways.

You need to know that:

Quarter **past** is the same as fifteen minutes past, so **quarter past three** is the same as **three fifteen**

Quarter to is the same as forty-five minutes past, so **quarter to three** is the same as **two forty-five**.

Quarter past eight is the same as eight fifteen

Quarter to five is the same as four forty-five

Ten to six is the same as five fifty

 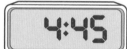 

Remember

Quarter past three is the same as **three fifteen**.

Quarter to three is the same as **two forty-five**.

1 Find the three pairs of clocks that show the same times:

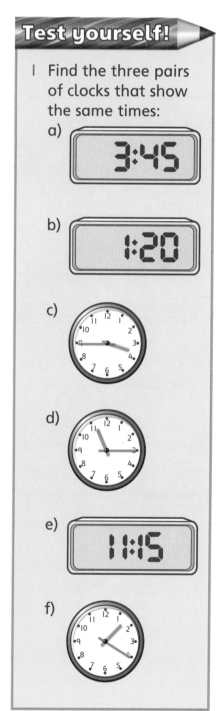

a) 3:45

b) 1:20

c)

d)

e) 11:15

f)

2-D shapes

2-D shapes are flat shapes without thickness.

Four different types of 2-D shapes

You need to know the names of these 2-D shapes and some things about them:

- Circle – one curved side

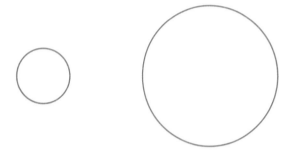

- Triangle – three straight sides

- Rectangle – four right angles and four straight sides

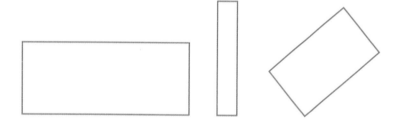

- Square – four right angles and four sides of equal length

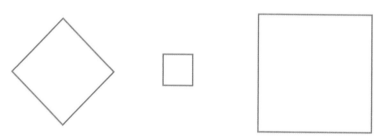

Remember

Circle – one curved side
Triangle – three straight sides
Rectangle – four right angles and four straight sides
Square – four right angles and four sides of equal length

2-D shapes

Three more types of 2-D shapes

Here are some more shapes that you need to know.

- Pentagon – five straight sides

- Hexagon – six straight sides

- Octagon – eight straight sides

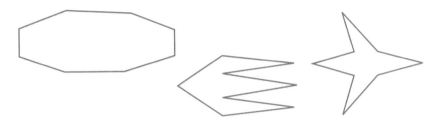

Test yourself!

1 Get a piece of paper, a ruler and a pencil. Cover the pictures of the shapes.
   Draw:
   a) an octagon
   b) a hexagon
   c) a pentagon

2 Which shape am I?
   I have:
   a) six straight sides
   b) eight straight sides
   c) five straight sides

Remember

Pentagon – five straight sides
Hexagon – six straight sides
Octagon – eight straight sides

Sorting shapes

We can sort shapes by looking at their sides and corners.

	number of sides	number of corners	straight or curved?
Circle	1	0	curved
Triangle	3	3	straight
Rectangle	4	4	straight
Square	4	4	straight
Pentagon	5	5	straight
Hexagon	6	6	straight
Octagon	8	8	straight

3-D shapes

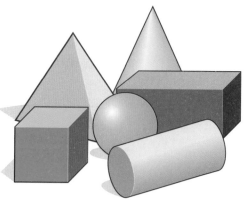

3-D shapes are solid shapes, that you can pick up, hold, or put something inside.

Six different types of 3-D shapes

You need to know the names of these 3-D shapes and some things about them.

3-D shapes with flat faces

A cube has square faces.

A cuboid has rectangular faces.

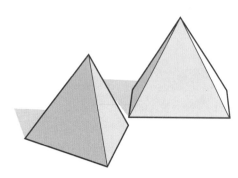

A pyramid has one face that can be any shape. All the other **faces** are **triangles** that meet together at a **point.**

3-D shapes with curved faces

A sphere is a ball.

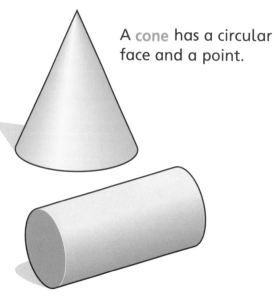

A cone has a circular face and a point.

A cylinder is like a tube with a circular face at each end.

Test yourself!

I Name these shapes:
a)

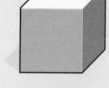

b)

c)

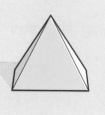

Remember

Some shapes have only **flat** faces, like **cubes**, **cuboids** or **pyramids**.

Some shapes have **curved** faces, like **spheres**, **cones** or **cylinders**.

3-D shapes

Faces, edges and corners

We can describe 3-D shapes by looking at the number of faces, edges and corners that each one has.

Faces are the surfaces making up the shape. They are 2-D shapes and can be flat or curved.

Edges are the lines where the faces meet. If you make a 3-D skeleton using straws, the straws are the edges of the shape.

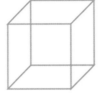

Corners are where the edges join together at a point.

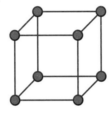

Cubes and cuboids

Cubes and cuboids have 6 flat faces (rectangular or square), 12 edges and 8 corners.

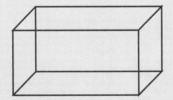

Sphere

A sphere has 1 curved face, no edges and no corners.

Cone

A cone has 1 circular flat face and 1 curved face. It has 1 edge and 1 corner.

Test yourself!

I Describe the faces, edges and corners of these shapes:

a)

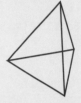

b)

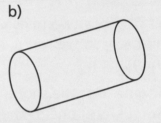

c)

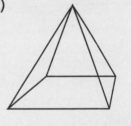

Remember

To help you remember the facts about 3-D shapes, try this activity.

First find some 3-D shapes around your home (such as a cornflake packet, a football and a toilet roll).

Then practise counting and describing the **faces**, **edges** and **corners**.

Symmetry

Symmetrical shapes and patterns

A shape or pattern is **symmetrical** when it has one or more lines of symmetry.
Look at the examples below.

Ink blot

This ink blot has **one line of symmetry**, so we say it is **symmetrical**.

Line of symmetry

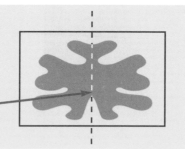

Flag

This flag has two **lines of symmetry** so we say it is **symmetrical**.

Imagine that the shape was folded along one of the lines. The two halves would match.

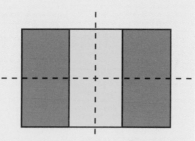

Cross

This cross has four **lines of symmetry** so we say it is **symmetrical**.

Imagine that the shape was folded along each of the lines. The two halves will always match!

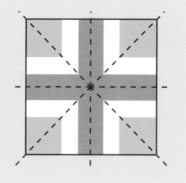

Cloud – a shape that is **not** symmetrical

This picture of a cloud is **different** from the shapes above.

Imagine it folded in half. Whichever way you fold it, the two halves do not match, so it is **not symmetrical**.

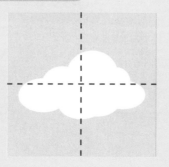

Test yourself!

I   Which of these patterns are symmetrical?

a)

b)

c)

d)

Remember

Imagine that the shape was **folded along a line**.

If it is a line of symmetry, the **two halves** will match.

Symmetry

Completing symmetrical patterns

Make this pattern symmetrical by colouring the squares on the other side of the mirror line

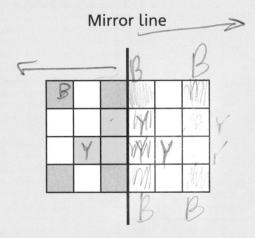

To complete the pattern, imagine that the coloured squares were wet ink or paint and that the paper was being folded along the mirror line. The wet paint would stick to the paper. Where would it end up?

Think your answer through like this:

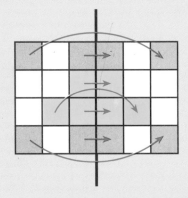

Check your pattern with a mirror

- Place the mirror along the mirror line.
- Look at the reflection in the mirror.
- Then lift the mirror out of the way and check that the reflection you have drawn is in the correct place.

Test yourself!

I Make these patterns symmetrical by colouring the circles.

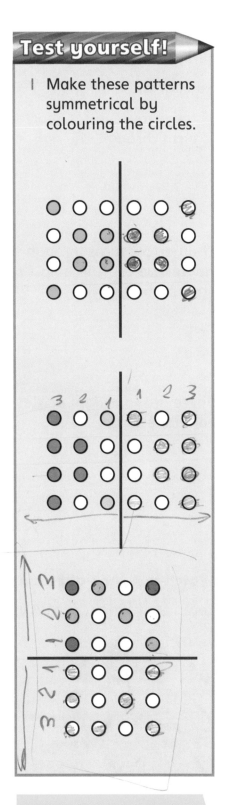

Remember

Check your pattern with a **mirror**.

Right angles and turns

Right angles

An angle is a part of a turn.

A right angle can also be called a quarter turn:

Look at these arrows ...

If the arrow turns a **quarter turn**, it turns through one **right angle**.

If an arrow turns through two **right angles** we call this a **half** turn or a straight line.

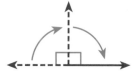

There are four **right angles** in a **complete turn**.

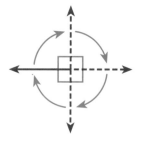

Watch out for right angles!

Learn to tick right angles in shapes like these ...

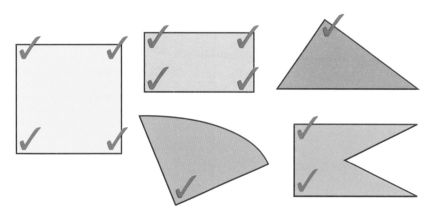

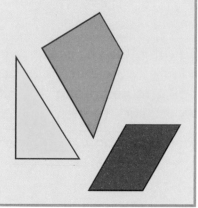

Test yourself!

1 How many right angles in a half turn?

2 How many right angles in a complete turn?

3 Tick any right angles in these shapes. Not every shape has a right angle.

Did you know?

The **outside corners of this page** are right angles. Look out for more of them around you, like at the edges of **doors** and **windows**.

Remember

A right angle is nothing to do with 'right' or left. It can be in any direction!

Positions

Describing positions

We describe positions using words like ...

lower than	higher than	beside
next to	below	above
to the left of	to the right of	underneath
at the corner of	on the edge of	between
opposite	close to	behind
in front of	inside	outside

How to remember left and right

If you find it difficult to remember your left from your right, think of the capital letter L.

Hold your hands out as if you were pushing something. Which hand makes the letter L?

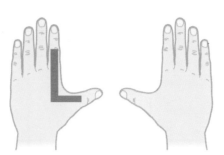

This is your left hand!

Describe where the kitten is in this picture, using some of the words in the boxes above

Answer: **underneath** the table, **to the right of** the person, **to the left of** the bin, **inside** the box

Test yourself!

I What item is:
  a) to the right of the cup?
  b) under the glove?
  c) to the left of the bell?
  d) below the shoe?
  e) between the phone and the pen?
  f) above the spoon?

Remember

Push away with your hands – the **left hand** shows the capital letter L.

Directions

Clockwise and anticlockwise

The hands of a clock turn
in a clockwise direction,
like this ...

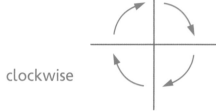

clockwise

The opposite to clockwise
is anticlockwise, like this...

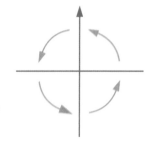

anticlockwise

The four compass points

This compass shows the four compass points,
North, South, East and West.

Ways to help you
remember the four
compass points:

'West – Left'

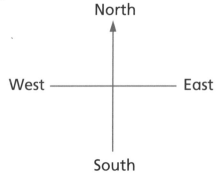

Go clockwise starting at North

Naughty Elephants Squirt Water
(North, East, South, West)

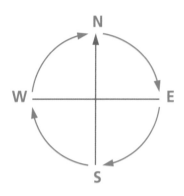

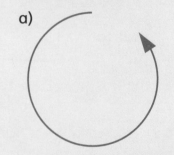
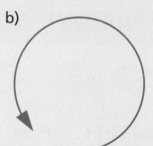
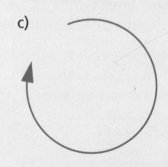
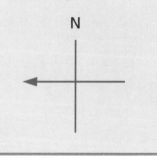
Remember

Naughty Elephants
Squirt Water!

Venn diagrams

We can use diagrams to help us to sort data.

Venn diagrams use a circle inside a rectangle, like this;

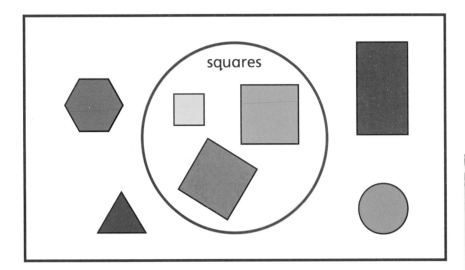

Sometimes two circles are used:

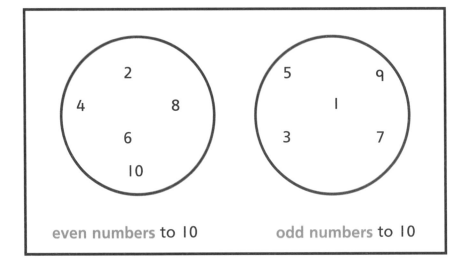

even numbers to 10   odd numbers to 10

Which of these shapes is in the wrong place?

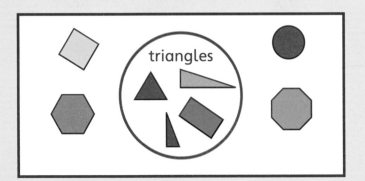

Answer: The rectangle is in the wrong place because it isn't a triangle.

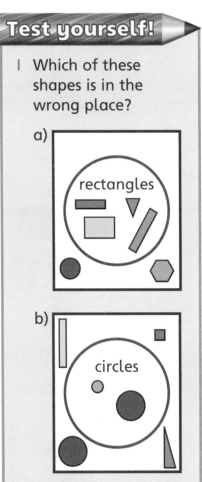

Test yourself!

I   Which of these shapes is in the wrong place?

a)

rectangles

b)

circles

Remember

We can use Venn diagrams to help us to sort data.

Venn diagrams use one or more circles inside a rectangle.

Carroll diagrams

A **Carroll diagram** is used for sorting data.

Carroll diagrams sort data inside rectangles. They always have something and its opposite, like 'red and not red' or 'even and not even'.

Carroll diagram showing multiples of 3 up to 30

even	not even
6 12	3 9
18 24	15 21
30	27

Carroll diagram showing shapes

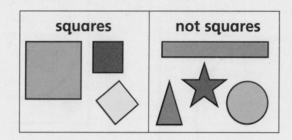

squares	not squares

Which of these numbers are in the wrong place?

Numbers up to 20

odd	not odd
7 11 5	6 18 12
9 15 19	14 13 2 20
1 3 17 8	10 4 16

Answer:

8 is in the wrong place because it is an even number (not odd).

13 is in the wrong place because it is an odd number.

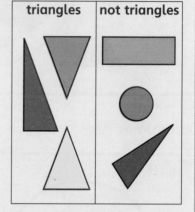
Remember

Carroll diagrams are made from **rectangles**.

They always show one type of thing and its **opposite**.

Tally charts

We can collect **data** and put it in a table.

To record data we can use **tallying**, like this **///**. Every line stands for one thing.

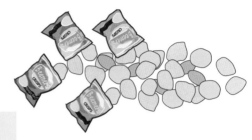

A tally chart of the favourite crisps of class 2

flavour	tally	total
Ready salted	////	4
Cheese and onion	///	3
Salt 'n vinegar	//////	6
Chicken	/////	5

In a tally chart showing how many bags of crisps we eat in a week, one line stands for one bag of crisps.

To make the tallies easier to count, we sometimes group them in fives, like this: ⊮

Can you see how the fifth tally is drawn across the other four to show a 'bundle of five'?

This means that the marks below show eight things

⊮ ///

   5 + 3 = 8

A tally chart of the pets of children in class 2

pet	tally	total
Hamster	///	3
Cat	⊮ ///	8
Dog	⊮ ⊮ /	11
Rabbit	////	4

Test yourself!

I Some children have been asked to say what their favourite zoo animal is.

Here are their answers:

lion	elephant
	tiger
lion	
	zebra tiger
lion	
	giraffe
zebra	tiger
zebra	tiger
giraffe	lion
tiger	elephant

Draw a tally chart of their answers.

Remember

To record data we can use **tallying**.

We sometimes group tallies in **fives** (four lines with a fifth line across them).

Pictograms

We can show the information on page 53 about the favourite crisps of children in class 2 on a pictogram.

A pictogram uses pictures of things, as in the examples below.

Pictogram of the favourite crisps of class 2

Ready salted   👤 👤 👤 👤

Cheese and onion   👤 👤 👤

Salt 'n vinegar   👤 👤 👤 👤 👤 👤

Chicken   👤 👤 👤 👤 👤

👤 = 1 child

Here is a pictogram of the pets of children in class 2, also using data from page 53.

Pictogram of the pets of children in class 2

Hamster   ☐☐☐

Cat   ☐☐☐☐☐☐☐☐

Dog   ☐☐☐☐☐☐☐☐☐☐

Rabbit   ☐☐☐☐

☐ = 1 child

How many children in class 2 have a cat?

Count the squares!

Answer: **8**

Test yourself!

1 Look at the pictogram of the favourite crisps of class 2. How many children chose:
   a) Ready salted?
   b) Salt 'n vinegar?

2 Look at the pictogram of the pets of children in class 2. How many children have:
   a) a hamster?
   b) a dog?

Remember

Pictograms use pictures of things to show information.

Block graphs

We can show the information on page 53 about the favourite crisps of children in class 2 as a block graph.

In a block graph, blocks are **joined up to make towers**, as in the examples below.

Block graph of the favourite crisps of class 2

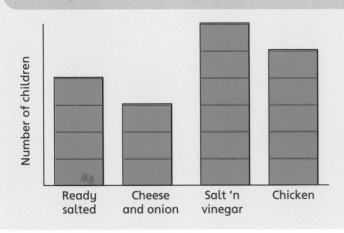

Block graph of pets of children in class 2

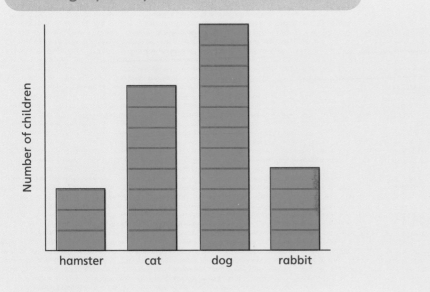

Test yourself!

1 Look at the block graph of the favourite crisps of class 2. How many children chose:
a) Cheese and onion?
b) Chicken?

2 Look at the block graph of the pets of children in class 2. How many children have:
a) a cat?
b) a rabbit?

Remember

Block graphs use **blocks joined up to make towers** to show information.

Answers

Page 4

1
a) Twelve
b) Twenty-four
c) Thirty-six
d) Eighty-four
e) Eighteen
f) Forty-eight
g) One hundred

2
a) 13
b) 60
c) 52
d) 76
e) 95
f) 11
g) 200

Page 5

1
a) even
b) odd
c) odd
d) even
e) even
f) odd
g) even
h) odd
i) even

2
123, 659, 597, 365, 471

Page 6

1 and 2
See number square on page 6.

3
a) 40, 41, 42
b) 69, 68, 67
c) 89, 90, 91
d) 96, 95, 94

Page 7

1
46, 48, 50, 52, 54, 56, 58, 60, 62, 64, 66, 68, 70, 72, 74, 76

2
53, 51, 49, 47, 45, 43, 41, 39, 37

3
a) 44, 46, 48
b) 67, 65, 63
c) 89, 91, 93
d) 92, 90, 88

Page 8

1 and 2
See number square on page 8.

3
a) 78, 88, 98
b) 59, 49, 39
c) 71, 81, 91
d) 84, 94, 104

Page 9

1
41, 46, 51, 56, 61, 66, 71, 76, 81, 86, 91, 96

2
48, 43, 38, 33, 28, 23, 18, 13, 8, 3

3
a) 58, 63, 68
b) 75, 70, 65
c) 67, 72, 77

Page 10

1
a) 9
b) 32, 42
c) 63, 59
d) 18, 33

Page 11

1 estimate close to 11
2 estimate close to 20

Page 12

1
a) 13, 39, 52, 64, 73
b) 21, 42, 47, 69, 79
c) 18, 57, 80, 81, 90

2
a) 5
b) 3
c) 9

3
a) 40 + 6
b) 80 + 4
c) 90 + 3
d) 30 + 7

Page 13

1
a) 193, 379, 572, 644, 743
b) 251, 411, 487, 629, 709

2
a) 5
b) 7
c) 2

3
a) 100 + 40 + 6
b) 400 + 30 + 9
c) 700 + 20 + 1
d) 200 + 90 + 7

Page 14

1 approximately 3, 15, 30, 30

Page 15

1 a) and d)

Page 16

1
a) $\frac{3}{4}$
b) $\frac{1}{4}$

2
a) $\frac{5}{10}$, which is the same as $\frac{1}{2}$
b) $\frac{9}{12}$, which is the same as $\frac{3}{4}$

Page 17

Yes, $\frac{1}{2}$ of the first piece is coloured in, and $\frac{1}{4} + \frac{1}{4}$ of the second piece is also coloured in ($\frac{1}{4} + \frac{1}{4} = \frac{1}{2}$).

Answers

Page 18

1

a) 20 + 9

b) 40 + 6

c) 70 + 8

2

a) 39

b) 41

c) 63

Page 19

1

a) 53

b) 68

c) 99

2

a) 245

b) 487

c) 902

3

a) 15

b) 18

c) 22

Page 20

1

a) 26

b) 22

c) 70

2

a) 17

b) 21

c) 25

d) 29

e) 39

Page 21

1

a) 35

b) 77

c) 76

d) 54

e) 112

Page 22

1

a) +

b) +

c) −

d) −

e) −

f) +

2

a) 41

b) 41

c) 46

Page 23

1

a) 57

b) 66

c) 79

2

a) 275

b) 503

c) 899

3

a) 5

b) 7

c) 7

d) 9

Page 24

1

a) 26

b) 27

c) 24

d) 18

e) 45

Page 25

1

a) 6

b) 1

c) 2

d) 7

2

a) 9

b) 16

c) 7

d) 8

3

a) 20

b) 60

c) 70

Page 26

1

a) 4 × 2

b) 4 × 5

c) 5 × 3

d) 3 × 4

e) 4 × 10

f) 4 × 3

g) 3 × 5

h) 5 × 2

Page 27

Check the answers against the multiplication tables on page 27.

Page 28

1

a) 2

b) 2

c) 3

d) 3

2

a) 5

b) 3

c) 4

d) 4

Page 29

Check the answers against the division tables on page 29.

Page 30

1

a) 16

b) 24

c) 12

d) 28

e) 18

f) 14

g) 26

h) 70

Answers

2
a) 11
b) 8
c) 25
d) 9
e) 35
f) 20
g) 45
h) 50

Page 31
1
a) 35 + 17 = 52
b) 7 × 2 = 14
c) 16 − 9 = 7
d) 20 ÷ 2 = 10

Page 32
1
a) 72p
b) 16
c) 15
d) 9

Page 33
1
a) for example 7 and 8
b) for example 9 and 6
2
a) for example 4 + 5 = 8 + 1
   or 4 + 1 = 5
b) for example 2 × 3 = 6
   or 6 ÷ 2 = 3

Page 34
1
a) 15p
b) 10p
c) 30p
d) 70p
e) 27p
f) £3
g) 66p
2
a) 50p + 5p + 2p + 2p
b) 50p + 20p + 5p + 2p + 1p
c) 20p + 10p + 2p + 2p
d) 50p + 10p + 2p + 1p

Page 35
1
a) 14p
b) 9p
c) 16p
d) 3p
2
a) 27p
b) 36p
c) 15p
d) 8p
e) 12p
f) 31p
g) 23p

Page 36
1
a) 3cm
b) 4cm
c) 7cm

Page 37
1
a) $4\frac{1}{2}$ kg
b) 350g

Page 38
1
a) 750ml
b) 600ml
c) 250ml

Page 39
1
a) 4:15
(quarter past four)
b) 4:30
(half past four)
c) 4:45
(quarter to five)

Page 40
1
a) 9:15
(quarter past nine)
b) 10:20
(twenty past ten)
c) 3:40
(twenty to four)

d) 9:25
(twenty-five past nine)
2
a) Wednesday
b) Sunday
3
a) April
b) July

Page 41
a) and c)
b) and f)
d) and e)

Page 42
1
Check the shapes against the pictures on page 42.
2
a) square
b) triangle
c) circle

Page 43
1
Check the shapes against the pictures on page 43.
2
a) hexagon
b) octagon
c) pentagon

Page 44
a) cube
b) sphere (ball)
c) pyramid

Page 45
1
a) 4 faces, 4 corners, 6 edges
b) 3 faces, 0 corners, 2 edges
c) 5 faces, 5 corners, 8 edges

Answers

Page 46

I

b), c) and d)

Page 47

This is how the patterns should look. It doesn't matter if the colours aren't exactly the same.

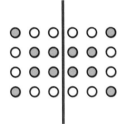

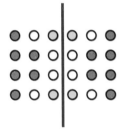

Page 48

I   2

2   4

3

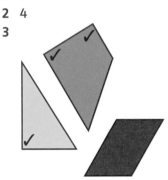

Page 49

I

a) pen

b) bell

c) cap

d) ball

e) cup

f) phone

Page 50

I

a) anticlockwise

b) anticlockwise

c) clockwise

2   West

Page 51

I

a) the green triangle inside the ring

b) There is a blue circle that should be inside the ring.

Page 52

I   There is a blue triangle in the 'not triangles' section.

2   33 and 34

Page 53

Animal	tally	total
Lion	IIII	4
Tiger	⊬IT	5
Elephant	II	2
Zebra	III	3
Giraffe	II	2

Page 54

I

a) 4

b) 6

2

a) 3

b) I I

Page 55

I

a) 3

b) 5

2

a) 8

b) 4

Curriculum chart

Primary National Strategy – Framework for mathematics

(Year 2 objectives, unless otherwise indicated)

Revision Guide

Counting and understanding number	Topic	Pages
Read and write two-digit and three-digit numbers in figures and words; describe and extend number sequences and recognise odd and even numbers	Numbers and their digits; Odd and even numbers	4, 5
Count up to 100 objects by grouping them and counting in tens, fives or twos; explain what each digit in a two-digit number represents, including numbers where 0 is a place holder; partition two-digit numbers in different ways, including into multiples of ten and one	Counting in ones, twos, tens and fives; Ordering	6, 7, 8, 9, 12
Order two-digit numbers and position them on a number line; use the greater than (>) and less than (<) signs	Number lines; Ordering	14 12
Partition three-digit numbers into multiples of one hundred, ten and one in different ways (Year 3)	Ordering	13
Estimate a number of objects; round two-digit numbers to the nearest 10	Estimating	11
Find one half, one quarter and three quarters of shapes and sets of objects	Fractions	15, 16, 17

Knowing and using number facts	Topic	Pages
Derive and recall all addition and subtraction facts for each number to at least 10, all pairs with totals to 20 and all pairs of multiples of 10 with totals up to 100	Addition and subtraction facts	25
Understand that halving is the inverse of doubling and derive and recall doubles of all numbers to 20, and the corresponding halves	Doubling and halving	30
Derive and recall multiplication facts for the 2, 5 and 10 times-tables and the related division facts; recognise multiples of 2, 5 and 10	Tables facts; Division facts	27 29
Use knowledge of number facts and operations to estimate and check answers to calculations	Addition and subtraction facts	25

Calculating	Topic	Pages
Add or subtract mentally a one-digit number or a multiple of 10 to or from any two-digit number; use practical and informal written methods to add and subtract two-digit numbers. Understand that subtraction is the inverse of addition and vice versa and use this to derive and record related addition and subtraction number sentences	Mental addition; Mental subtraction	18, 19, 20, 21, 22, 23, 24
Represent repeated addition and arrays as multiplication, and sharing and repeated subtraction (grouping) as division; use practical and informal written methods and related vocabulary to support multiplication and division, including calculations with remainders	Multiplication Division	26 28
Use the symbols +, −, ×, ÷ and = to record and interpret number sentences involving all four operations; calculate the value of an unknown in a number sentence (e.g. □ ÷ 2 = 6, 30 − □ = 24)	Number stories	31

Using and applying mathematics	Topic	Pages
Solve problems involving addition, subtraction, multiplication or division in contexts of numbers, measures or pounds and pence	Number stories; Money	31 34, 35
Identify and record the information or calculation needed to solve a puzzle or problem; carry out the steps or calculations and check the solution in the context of the problem	Number problems	32, 33
Follow a line of enquiry; answer questions by choosing and using suitable equipment and selecting, organising and presenting information in lists, tables and simple diagrams	Tally charts	53
Describe patterns and relationships involving numbers or shapes, make predictions and test these with examples	Number patterns	10
Present solutions to puzzles and problems in an organised way; explain decisions, methods and results in pictorial, spoken or written form, using mathematical language and number sentences	Pictograms	54

Curriculum chart

Primary National Strategy – Framework for mathematics

(Year 2 objectives, unless otherwise indicated)

Revision Guide

Measuring

	Topic	Pages
Estimate, compare and measure lengths, weights and capacities, choosing and using standard units (m, cm, kg, litre) and suitable measuring instruments	Length; Mass; Capacity	36, 37 38
Read the numbered divisions on a scale, and interpret the divisions between them (e.g. on a scale from 0 to 25 with intervals of 1 shown but only the divisions 0, 5, 10, 15 and 20 numbered); use a ruler to draw and measure lines to the nearest centimetre	Length; Mass; Capacity	36, 37 38
Use units of time (seconds, minutes, hours, days) and know the relationships between them; read the time to the quarter hour; identify time intervals, including those that cross the hour	Time	39, 40, 41

Understanding shape

	Topic	Pages
Visualise common 2-D shapes and 3-D solids; identify shapes from pictures of them in different positions and orientations; sort, make and describe shapes, referring to their properties	2-D shapes; 3-D shapes	42, 43 44, 45
Identify reflective symmetry in patterns and 2-D shapes and draw lines of symmetry in shapes	Symmetry	46, 47
Follow and give instructions involving position, direction and movement	Positions	49
Recognise and use whole, half and quarter turns, both clockwise and anticlockwise; know that a right angle represents a quarter turn	Right angles and turns	48
Read and record the vocabulary of position, direction and movement, using the four compass directions to describe movement about a grid (Year 3)	Directions	50

Handling data

	Topic	Pages
Answer a question by collecting and recording data in lists and tables; represent the data as block graphs or pictograms to show results; use ICT to organise and present data	Tally charts; Pictograms; Block graphs	53 54 55
Use lists, tables and diagrams to sort objects; explain choices using appropriate language, including 'not'	Tally charts; Pictograms; Block graphs	53 54 55
Use Venn diagrams or Carroll diagrams to sort data and objects using more than one criterion (Year 3)	Venn diagrams; Carroll diagrams	51 52

Glossary

2-D shapes	flat shapes without thickness
3-D shapes	solid or hollow shapes that you can pick up or hold
addition	joining together numbers or things to make totals. These are all words that can mean addition: more, add, plus, sum, total, altogether, and. This sign means addition +.
angle	part of a turn
anticlockwise	the opposite direction to clockwise
block graph	a type of graph that uses blocks joined together to show data
calculation	working out
capacity	how much something holds. We measure capacity in millilitres (ml) and litres (l).
Carroll diagrams	special diagrams that help us to sort data. They always have something and its opposite, like 'red' and 'not red' or 'even' and 'not even'.
circle	a 2-D shape with one curved side
clockwise	the hands of a clock turn in a clockwise direction
cone	a 3-D shape with a circular face and a point
corners	the place where the edges of a 3-D shape join together at a point
cube	a 3-D shape with square faces
cuboid	a 3-D shape with rectangular faces
cylinder	a 3-D shape like a tube with a circular face at each end
data	information
digits	the 10 symbols we use to write numbers (0, 1, 2, 3, 4, 5, 6, 7, 8 and 9)
division	sharing or sorting things into equal groups
doubling	multiplying by 2
edges	the lines where the faces of a 3-D shape meet. If you make the skeleton of a 3-D shape using straws, the straws are the edges of the shape.
estimate	to make a 'good guess'
even number	any number that is divided by 2 without a remainder. All even numbers end in 0, 2, 4, 6 or 8.
faces	the surfaces that make up a 3-D shape. Faces are 2-D shapes and can be flat or curved.
fraction	part of something that has been split into equal parts
half	one part of something split into two equal parts
hexagon	a 2-D shape with six straight sides
length	how long something is. We measure length in centimetres and metres.
mass	how heavy an object is. Mass is measured in grams (g) and kilograms (kg).

Glossary

multiple	a number that is in a times table. Multiples of 3 are 3, 6, 9, 12, 15, 18, 21, 24, 27, 30, 33, 36, 39 and they carry on and on in threes.
multiplication	a quick way of adding the same number many times. The sign × means multiplication.
octagon	a 2-D shape with eight straight sides
odd number	any number that, when divided by 2, has a remainder of 1. All odd numbers end in 1, 3, 5, 7 or 9.
pentagon	a 2-D shape with five straight sides
pictogram	diagrams used to show data. They use pictures of things.
pyramid	a 3-D shape with one face that can be any shape and all the other faces are triangles that meet together at a point
quarter	one part of something split into four equal parts
rectangle	a 2-D shape with four right angles and four straight sides
remainder	what is left over when one number is divided by another number
right angle	a quarter turn. There are four right angles in a full turn.
sequence	numbers arranged in a special order
sphere	a 3-D shape that is like a ball
square	a 2-D shape with four right angles and four sides of equal length
subtraction	taking away part of a group of things or a number. These are all words that can mean subtraction: subtract, take away, less than, minus, difference between, fewer. This sign − means subtraction.
tallying	a way of recording data with lines like this. /// Each line stands for one of the things being counted. Sometimes tallying is used to make a tally chart.
triangle	a 2-D shape with three straight sides
symmetry	a shape has symmetry (is symmetrical) when it is the same on both sides of a line
Venn diagrams	diagrams using circles inside a rectangle. They help us to sort data.

Index